Flute

101 JAZZ SONGS

Available for
**FLUTE, CLARINET, ALTO SAX, TENOR SAX, TRUMPET,
HORN, TROMBONE, VIOLIN, VIOLA, CELLO**

ISBN 978-1-4950-2336-1

Hal•Leonard®
CORPORATION

7777 W. BLUEMOUND RD. P.O. BOX 13819 MILWAUKEE, WI 53213

Visit Hal Leonard Online at
www.halleonard.com

CONTENTS

ALL OF ME

Flute

Words and Music by SEYMOUR SIMONS
and GERALD MARKS

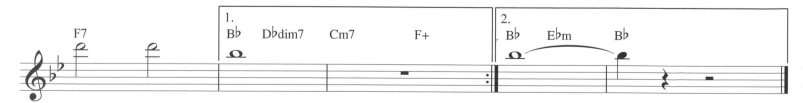

ALL THE THINGS YOU ARE

Flute

Lyrics by OSCAR HAMMERSTEIN II
Music by JEROME KERN

APRIL IN PARIS

Flute

Words by E.Y. "YIP" HARBURG
Music by VERNON DUKE

AUTUMN IN NEW YORK

Flute

Words and Music by
VERNON DUKE

AUTUMN LEAVES

FLUTE

English Lyric by JOHNNY MERCER
French Lyric by JACQUES PREVERT
Music by JOSEPH KOSMA

BEWITCHED

Words by LORENZ HART
Music by RICHARD RODGERS

Flute

BEYOND THE SEA

Lyrics by JACK LAWRENCE
Music by CHARLES TRENET and ALBERT LASRY
Original French Lyric to "La Mer" by CHARLES TRENET

Flute

THE BLUE ROOM

Flute

Words by LORENZ HART
Music by RICHARD RODGERS

BLUE SKIES

flute

Words and Music by
IRVING BERLIN

BLUESETTE

Flute

Words by NORMAN GIMBEL
Music by JEAN THIELEMANS

BODY AND SOUL

Flute

Words by EDWARD HEYMAN,
ROBERT SOUR and FRANK EYTON
Music by JOHN GREEN

Moderately slow, with a lilt

BUT BEAUTIFUL

Words by JOHNNY BURKE
Music by JIMMY VAN HEUSEN

Flute

CAN'T HELP LOVIN' DAT MAN

Flute

Lyrics by OSCAR HAMMERSTEIN II
Music by JEROME KERN

CARAVAN

Flute

Words and Music by DUKE ELLINGTON,
IRVING MILLS and JUAN TIZOL

CHARADE

Flute

By HENRY MANCINI

CHEEK TO CHEEK

Flute

Words and Music by
IRVING BERLIN

COME RAIN OR COME SHINE

Flute

Words by JOHNNY MERCER
Music by HAROLD ARLEN

DANCING ON THE CEILING

Flute

Words by LORENZ HART
Music by RICHARD RODGERS

DEARLY BELOVED

Flute

Music by JEROME KERN
Words by JOHNNY MERCER

DO NOTHIN' TILL YOU HEAR FROM ME

Flute

Words and Music by DUKE ELLINGTON
and BOB RUSSELL

DON'T GET AROUND MUCH ANYMORE

Flute

Words and Music by DUKE ELLINGTON
and BOB RUSSELL

DREAMSVILLE

Flute

By HENRY MANCINI

FALLING IN LOVE WITH LOVE

Flute

Words by LORENZ HART
Music by RICHARD RODGERS

A FINE ROMANCE

Flute

Words by DOROTHY FIELDS
Music by JEROME KERN

FLY ME TO THE MOON
(In Other Words)

Flute

Words and Music by
BART HOWARD

GEORGIA ON MY MIND

Flute

Words by STUART GORRELL
Music by HOAGY CARMICHAEL

HERE'S THAT RAINY DAY

Flute

Words by JOHNNY BURKE
Music by JIMMY VAN HEUSEN

HERE'S TO LIFE

Flute

Music by ARTIE BUTLER
Lyrics by PHYLLIS MOLINARY

HONEYSUCKLE ROSE

Flute

Words by ANDY RAZAF
Music by THOMAS "FATS" WALLER

Moderately, with a lilt

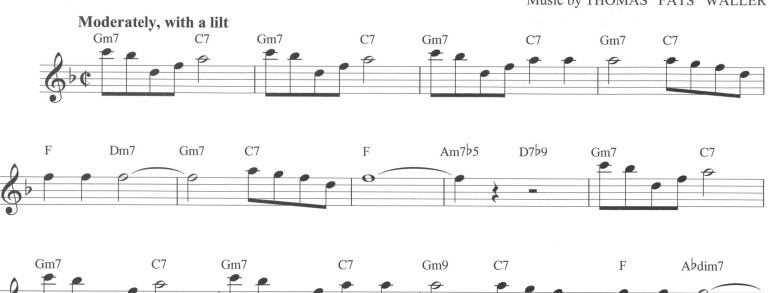

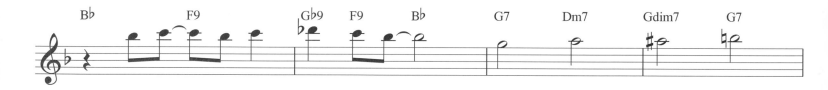

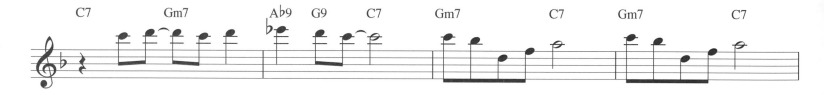

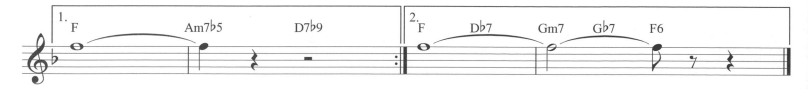

HOW DEEP IS THE OCEAN
(How High Is the Sky)

Flute

Words and Music by
IRVING BERLIN

HOW INSENSITIVE
(Insensatez)

Music by ANTONIO CARLOS JOBIM
Original Words by VINICIUS DE MORAES
English Words by NORMAN GIMBEL

Flute

Medium Bossa Nova

I CAN'T GET STARTED

Flute

Words by IRA GERSHWIN
Music by VERNON DUKE

I COULD WRITE A BOOK

Flute

Words by LORENZ HART
Music by RICHARD RODGERS

I GOT IT BAD AND THAT AIN'T GOOD

Flute

Words by PAUL FRANCIS WEBSTER
Music by DUKE ELLINGTON

I'LL REMEMBER APRIL

Flute

Words and Music by PAT JOHNSTON,
DON RAYE AND GENE DE PAUL

I'M BEGINNING TO SEE THE LIGHT

Flute

Words and Music by DON GEORGE, JOHNNY HODGES,
DUKE ELLINGTON and HARRY JAMES

I'VE GOT THE WORLD ON A STRING

Flute

Words by TED KOEHLER
Music by HAROLD ARLEN

IF I WERE A BELL

Flute

By FRANK LOESSER

IMAGINATION

Flute

Words by JOHNNY BURKE
Music by JIMMY VAN HEUSEN

Slowly, with a lilt

IN A SENTIMEMTAL MOOD

Flute

By DUKE ELLINGTON

IN THE WEE SMALL HOURS OF THE MORNING

Words by BOB HILLIARD
Music by DAVID MANN

Flute

INDIANA
(Back Home Again in Indiana)

Flute

Words by BALLARD MacDONALD
Music by JAMES F. HANLEY

ISN'T IT ROMANTIC?

Words by LORENZ HART
Music by RICHARD RODGERS

Flute

IT COULD HAPPEN TO YOU

Flute

Words by JOHNNY BURKE
Music by JAMES VAN HEUSEN

IT DON'T MEAN A THING
(If It Ain't Got That Swing)

Flute

Words and Music by DUKE ELLINGTON
and IRVING MILLS

IT MIGHT AS WELL BE SPRING

Lyrics by OSCAR HAMMERSTEIN II
Music by RICHARD RODGERS

Flute

THE LADY IS A TRAMP

Words by LORENZ HART
Music by RICHARD RODGERS

LAZY RIVER

Flute

Words and Music by HOAGY CARMICHAEL
and SIDNEY ARODIN

LET THERE BE LOVE

Flute

Lyric by IAN GRANT
Music by LIONEL RAND

LIKE SOMEONE IN LOVE

Flute

Words by JOHNNY BURKE
Music by JIMMY VAN HEUSEN

LITTLE GIRL BLUE

Flute

Words by LORENZ HART
Music by RICHARD RODGERS

LONG AGO (AND FAR AWAY)

Flute

Words by IRA GERSHWIN
Music by JEROME KERN

LOVER, COME BACK TO ME

Flute

Lyrics by OSCAR HAMMERSTEIN II
Music by SIGMUND ROMBERG

Moderately

LULLABY OF BIRDLAND

Flute

Words by GEORGE DAVID WEISS
Music by GEORGE SHEARING

LULLABY OF THE LEAVES

FLUTE

Words by JOE YOUNG
Music by BERNICE PETKERE

MANHATTAN

Flute

Words by LORENZ HART
Music by RICHARD RODGERS

MEDITATION
(Meditação)

Music by ANTONIO CARLOS JOBIM
Original Words by NEWTON MENDONÇA
English Words by NORMAN GIMBEL

Flute

Medium Bossa Nova

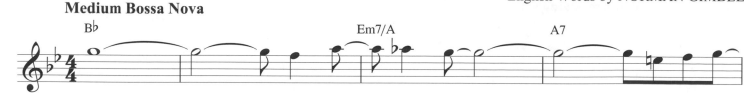

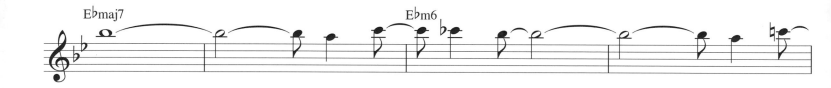

MIDNIGHT SUN

Words and Music by LIONEL HAMPTON,
SONNY BURKE and JOHNNY MERCER

Flute

MISTY

Flute

Music by ERROLL GARNER

MOOD INDIGO

Flute

Words and Music by DUKE ELLINGTON,
IRVING MILLS and ALBANY BIGARD

Moderately slow

MOONLIGHT IN VERMONT

Flute

Words by JOHN BLACKBURN
Music by KARL SUESSDORF

MORE THAN YOU KNOW

Flute

Words by WILLIAM ROSE and EDWARD ELISCU
Music by VINCENT YOUMANS

Slowly, with expression

MY HEART STOOD STILL

Words by LORENZ HART
Music by RICHARD RODGERS

Flute

MY OLD FLAME

Flute

Words and Music by ARTHUR JOHNSTON
and SAM COSLOW

MY ONE AND ONLY LOVE

Flute

Words by ROBERT MELLIN
Music by GUY WOOD

MY ROMANCE

Flute

Words by LORENZ HART
Music by RICHARD RODGERS

MY SHIP

Flute

Words by IRA GERSHWIN
Music by KURT WEILL

THE NEARNESS OF YOU

Flute

Words by NED WASHINGTON
Music by HOAGY CARMICHAEL

A NIGHT IN TUNISIA

Flute

By JOHN "DIZZY" GILLESPIE
and FRANK PAPARELLI

ON GREEN DOLPHIN STREET

Flute

Lyrics by NED WASHINGTON
Music by BRONISLAU KAPER

ONE NOTE SAMBA

(Samba de uma nota so)

Flute

Original Lyrics by NEWTON MENDONÇA
English Lyrics by ANTONIO CARLOS JOBIM
Music by ANTONIO CARLOS JOBIM

Medium Bossa Nova

PICK YOURSELF UP

Flute

Words by DOROTHY FIELDS
Music by JEROME KERN

POLKA DOTS AND MOONBEAMS

Flute

Words by JOHNNY BURKE
Music by JIMMY VAN HEUSEN

QUIET NIGHTS OF QUIET STARS
(Corcovado)

Flute

English Words by GENE LEES
Original Words and Music by ANTONIO CARLOS JOBIM

Medium Bossa Nova

SATIN DOLL

Flute

By DUKE ELLINGTON

SKYLARK

Flute

Words by JOHNNY MERCER
Music by HOAGY CARMICHAEL

Moderate Swing

SO NICE
(Summer Samba)

Flute

Original Words and Music by MARCOS VALLE
and PAULO SERGIO VALLE
English Words by NORMAN GIMBEL

Medium Bossa Nova

SOPHISTICATED LADY

Flute

Words and Music by DUKE ELLINGTON,
IRVING MILLS and MITCHELL PARISH

SPEAK LOW

Flute

Words by OGDEN NASH
Music by KURT WEILL

STELLA BY STARLIGHT

Words by NED WASHINGTON
Music by VICTOR YOUNG

Flute

STOMPIN' AT THE SAVOY

Flute

By BENNY GOODMAN,
EDGAR SAMPSON and CHICK WEBB

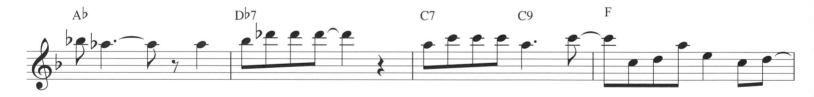

STORMY WEATHER
(Keeps Rainin' All the Time)

Flute

Lyric by TED KOEHLER
Music by HAROLD ARLEN

A SUNDAY KIND OF LOVE

Flute

Words and Music by LOUIS PRIMA, ANITA NYE LEONARD,
STANLEY RHODES and BARBARA BELLE

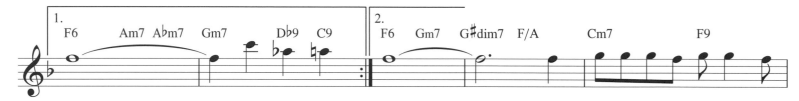

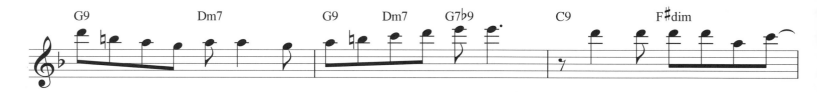

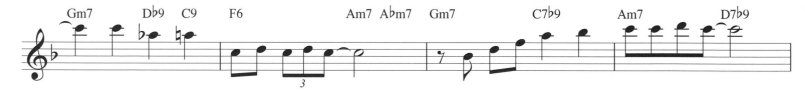

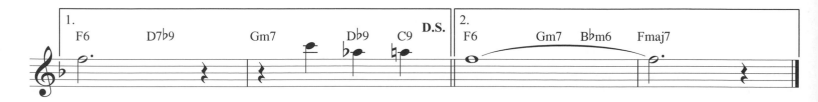

Tangerine

Flute

Words by JOHNNY MERCER
Music by VICTOR SCHERTZINGER

THERE'S A SMALL HOTEL

Words by LORENZ HART
Music by RICHARD RODGERS

Flute

THESE FOOLISH THINGS (REMIND ME OF YOU)

Flute

Words by HOLT MARVELL
Music by JACK STRACHEY

THE THINGS WE DID LAST SUMMER

Flute

Words by SAMMY CAHN
Music by JULE STYNE

This Can't Be Love

Flute

Words by LORENZ HART
Music by RICHARD RODGERS

Moderately

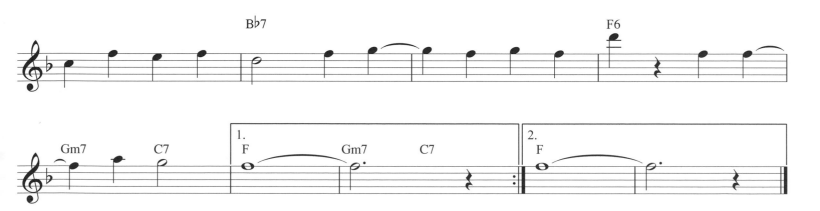

THOU SWELL

Words by LORENZ HART
Music by RICHARD RODGERS

Flute

UNFORGETTABLE

Flute

Words and Music by
IRVING GORDON

THE VERY THOUGHT OF YOU

Flute

Words and Music by
RAY NOBLE

WATCH WHAT HAPPENS

Music by MICHEL LEGRAND
Original French Text by JACQUES DEMY
English Lyrics by NORMAN GIMBEL

Flute

WAVE

Words and Music by
ANTONIO CARLOS JOBIM

Flute

Medium Bossa Nova

THE WAY YOU LOOK TONIGHT

Flute

Words by DOROTHY FIELDS
Music by JEROME KERN

WHAT'LL I DO

FLUTE

Words and Music by
IRVING BERLIN

WILLOW WEEP FOR ME

Flute

Words and Music by
ANN RONELL

WITCHCRAFT

Music by CY COLEMAN
Lyrics by CAROLYN LEIGH

Moderately

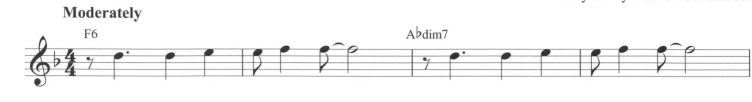

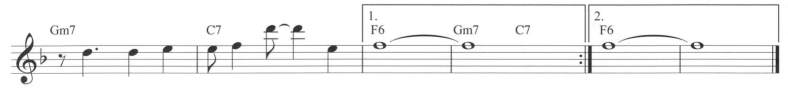

YESTERDAYS

Words by OTTO HARBACH
Music by JEROME KERN

Flute

YOU ARE TOO BEAUTIFUL

Flute

Words by LORENZ HART
Music by RICHARD RODGERS

YOU BROUGHT A NEW KIND OF LOVE TO ME

Flute

Words and Music by SAMMY FAIN,
IRVING KAHAL and PIERRE NORMAN

Medium Swing

YOU DON'T KNOW WHAT LOVE IS

Flute

Words and Music by DON RAYE
and GENE DePAUL